The American Natives – Still Marching on the Trail of Tears

Contents

Disclaimer..3

Introduction 5

Mistreatment by the legal system 12

Lack of prosecution and crime rates................22

Substance abuse 33

Sexual abuse and violence 45

Poverty 52

Disclaimer

Copyright © 2018

All Rights Reserved.

No part of this book can be transmitted or reproduced in any form including print, electronic, photocopying, scanning, mechanical, or recording without a prior written permission of the author.

While the author has taken utmost efforts to ensure the accuracy of the written content, all readers are advised to follow information mentioned herein at their own risk. The author cannot be held responsible for any personal or commercial damage caused by the misinterpretation of information. All readers are encouraged to seek professional advice when needed.

This book has been written for informational purposes only. Every effort has been made to make this book as complete and accurate as possible. However, the author does not make any warranties whatsoever regarding the accuracy and completeness of the information present within this book.

The purpose of this book is to educate. The author and the publisher do not warrant that the information contained in this book is complete and error-free and shall not be responsible for any errors, omissions, or dated information. The author and publisher shall have neither liability nor responsibility to any person or entity with respect to any loss or damage caused or alleged to be caused directly or indirectly by this e-book.

Introduction

This book has been written to present a broad outline of the injustices that the Native American / Native Indian community faces while living in the United States. Each chapter represents an aspect of the mistreatment that Native Indians face.

The first chapter talks about how flaws in the legal system have led to a bias against the average Native Indian. The issue of Native Indians being dealt harsher punishments, for crimes committed compared to other American citizens, has been raised a countless number of times. According to data compiled by the US Sentencing Commission:

- Statistics compiled by the Bureau of Justice Statistics reveal that the rate at which Native Indians face incarceration is 38% higher than the national average.
- According to the National Council on Crime and Delinquency, the likelihood of Native Indian youths being sentenced to juvenile court rather have charges dropped against them is 30% greater, compared to other Americans.
- According to statistical data compiled by the Center on Juvenile and Criminal Justice, Native Indians have a greater

likelihood of being killed by the police compared to any other racial group.

- In a report prepared by Lakota People's Law Project, the rate at which Native Indian men face incarceration is four times higher than that for white men. For Native American women, the incarceration rate is six times than that for white women.
- The rate of violent crime against Native Indians is more than two times the rate of violent crime against other US citizens, according to reports prepared by the BJS. Moreover, 88% of violent crimes to which Native Indian women have fallen to, were carried out by people who were non-Native.

The second chapter discusses how acts of crime on Native Indian reservations have a significantly lower rate of prosecution by attorneys of the United States. The Justice Department, which has the responsibility for the prosecution of crimes of the most severe degree, has been observed to file charges for only half the murders that take place on Indian reservations. It has also been observed that almost 66% of the cases involving sexual assault are turned down. These observations emerged in the light of new federal data compilations.

According to the data accumulated by the Justice Department, the rate of violent crimes within the 310 Indian reservations is greater than two and a half times, compared to national averages. The data further reveals that the likelihood of Native Indian women being murdered is 10 times more, compared to that of other Americans. The rate of rape or sexual assault is four times that of the national average. More than 33% of the time, Indian women have experienced either rape or an attempt at rape.

The third chapter discusses the problem of substance abuse on the reservations. According to numerous reports, the abuse of alcohol, drugs and even cigarettes is far higher on Indian reservations compared to national averages. Native American youths have been observed to have higher rates of drug abuse and alcoholism compared to many other ethnic or racial groups. Further data reveals that the individuals who live on the reservations have the highest risk of developing problems related to consuming alcohol. The Kunitz study on alcoholism in the Native Indian populace is a popular and well known one. The study shows that the reason why alcohol consumption and alcoholism are so prevalent is that acquiring alcohol is much easier. Furthermore, the consumption levels that were not problematic in the past have led to consequences in the form of mortality and morbidity. Hence the consumption and subsequent addiction is particularly present on reservations. Yet another reason is the advertising and how alcohol and beer distributors and manufacturers have contributed to the spread.

The fourth chapter discusses the rampant sexual abuse on Indian reservations. Startling statistics have come to light through a study conducted by the Department of Justice. 2,000 women were surveyed in this study. 84% of Alaskan and American Native women suffered from violence, 56% of them were prey to sexual violence and more than 90% fell prey to violence by a non-tribal member. Most of the women were fearful for their safety and approximately half of them had suffered generic physical violence like being beaten, being shoved or pushed. Over 60% had experienced coercive or emotional abuse. Experts are still of the opinion that the numbers are still understating the number of women that are actually affected by violence. Reporting structures and institutions are underfunded.

Finally, the fifth chapter talks about the prevalence of poverty on the Indian reservations. The official poverty rate for Native Indians in the United States living on reservations is 29.4%. The national average poverty rate is 15.3%. The poverty rate for native Indian households on reservations is 36%. The national average poverty rate is 9.2%.

Mistreatment by the legal system

This chapter deals with the injustices that Native Indians face in terms of the sentencing that they receive from the American legal system for committing crimes. Given the scope of the book, the idea is to present a broad overview of how this is happening.

The mistreatment of Native Indians by the legal system is not a recent issue. Several judges over the years have raised concerns about the flaws present in the legal system.

In April 2015, The Wall Street Journal conducted an interview with Ralph Erickson, who is a chief federal district court judge for North Dakota. Erickson has been an outspoken advocate for reforms in how sentencing happens on Native Indian reservations. He is now leading a federal review of the US legal system that deals with administering punishments on Indian reservations. The review is called the Tribal Issues Advisory Group and comprises of 22 law enforcement officials and judges, out of which 11 are Native Indian.

Erickson, in his interview, spoke of the times that he had been asked about why Indians received harsher sentences, by family members of people whom he had convicted. "No matter how long I have been sentencing in Indian Country, I find it gut-wrenching when I am asked by a family member of a person I have sentenced why Indians are sentenced to longer sentences than white people who commit the same crime," he said.

One such example is the conviction of Gerald James Viarrial, a member of the Pojoaque Pueblo tribe. He has been charged with assault and the possession and use of firearms. The incident occurred at a pueblo, which meant that it came under federal jurisdiction. The punishment that Viarrial faces is forty years for the charge of assault and at least seven years for the charge of firearms. Had the conviction occurred through the state court of New Mexico, the minimum mandatory sentence for the firearms charge would have been one year, and the sentence for the assault charge would not have been more than six years.

One of the major reasons why this happens is that Native Indians are prosecuted by federal law for committing serious crimes on reservations. Corresponding punishments under state laws are usually lighter.

According to Samuel Winder, who is a member of the Southern Ute tribe, this disparity is a result of the Major Crimes Act of 1885. Congress passed this act after there was a dispute over deciding the jurisdiction for crimes that were committed on Native Indian reservations.

"Crow Dog" who was a Sioux man, was convicted for the murder of Chief Spotted Tail. Chief Spotted Tail had been shot and murdered in August 1881. Crow Dog's lawyers had presented the argument that the courts did not have jurisdiction over crimes that were committed by Indians against Indians on land that was owned by Indians. The U.S. Supreme Court had agreed and as a result, Congress had then passed the Major Crimes Act, under which Indians were to be tried in a federal court if they committed a felony crime within reservations.

According to the Journal, the US Sentencing Commission had authorized a similar review over a decade ago. The discrepancies had come to light since then, however there weren't any tangible changes after the review had published its findings. Over more than the last five years, there has been an increase of 27% in the number of Native Indians that have been incarcerated and sentenced to federal prisons. In South Dakota, the state which houses the fourth highest number of Native Indians, 60% of the crime cases involve Native Indians. It is pertinent to note that they comprise only 8.5% of the total state population.

This trend is observed in a number of states that house sizeable Native Indian populations. The statistics for the respective federal caseloads are as under:

- 33% in Montana

- 25% in North Dakota
- 14% in Minnesota
- 13% in Oklahoma

This information is in accordance with data compiled by the US Sentencing Commission.

These statistics unfortunately merely represent the reality at a surface level. Studies that breakdown criminal punishment and incarceration from a racial aspect, reveal that Native Indians are, at the very least, overrepresented in US prisons and jails. However, media coverage and scholarly reviews of the inequality are few in number.

- Statistics compiled by the Bureau of Justice Statistics reveal that the rate at which Native Indians face incarceration is 38% higher than the national average.

- According to the National Council on Crime and Delinquency, the likelihood of Native Indian youths being sentenced to juvenile court rather have charges dropped against them is 30% greater, compared to other Americans.
- According to statistical data compiled by the Center on Juvenile and Criminal Justice, Native Indians have a greater likelihood of being killed by the police compared to any other racial group.
- In a report prepared by Lakota People's Law Project, the rate at which Native Indian men face incarceration is four times higher than that for white men. For Native American women, the

incarceration rate is six times than that for white women.

- The rate of violent crime against Native Indians is more than two times the rate of violent crime against other US citizens, according to reports prepared by the BJS. Moreover, 88% of violent crimes to which Native Indian women have fallen to, were carried out by people who were non-Native.

The majority of felony crimes that Native Indians commit are dealt under federal law, which does increase the severity of the punishment that the crimes entail. However the sheer racial disparity in incarceration is not merely the product of a few differences between state and federal legislature; that is an oversimplification of the problem.

Several American minorities lack a lot of communitarian infrastructure that is crucial for mitigating the prevalence of crime. This deprivation is particularly evident in the case of Native Indians. In this regard, the federal government can take tangible steps for resolving the gross overrepresentation in juvenile correction systems and US prisons, by funneling funds into the establishment of child and family services on reservations. Tribal juvenile centers along with substance rehabilitation centers can also be setup in this regard. (According to the Lakota People's Law Project ('LPLP') 70% of Native Indians who have been convicted of violent crimes have claimed that they had been drinking at the time they had committed the crime.)

Lack of prosecution and crime rates

Native Indian reservations all over the US have suffered from high rates of crime over years. These crime rates are only rivaled by a few cities in the nation, where crime is most prevalent. However, the Justice Department, which has the responsibility of prosecuting the most severe reservation related crimes, has only filed charges for approximately half of the murder investigations within Native Indian territory. The Department has also refused to handle almost 66% of the cases pertaining to sexual assault. This information is in light of recently compiled federal data.

According to the data accumulated by the Justice Department, the rate of violent crimes within the 310 Indian reservations is greater than two and a half times, compared to national averages. The data further reveals that the likelihood of Native Indian women being murdered is 10 times more, compared to that of other Americans. The rate of rape or sexual assault is four times that of the national average. More than 33% of the time, Indian women have experienced either rape or an attempt at rape.

Various tribes have raised the issue of the lower rate of prosecution by FBI officials and agents, and US attorneys of the crimes, as it is their responsibility to prosecute the most serious criminal offenses on reservations. The tribes call the justice system a second class system that effectively encourages breaking the law. The prosecutors contend this by giving the reason that there is a lack of evidence that is admissible.

According to Brendan Johnson who is a United States attorney for all reservations in South Dakota, the government had recently positioned extra FBI agents and prosecutors in Native Indian land. The Justice Department has stated that it is looking to make its rulings more transparent. Mr. Johnson said the discontentment of the Indians on the reservations was understandable. He admitted that he would be also be irritated if the rate of crime in his community was like that as well.

However the tribes have a further bone of contention which is not being informed by the government of the reason why cases on the reservation aren't taken up and addressed.

According to Jerry Gardner who works with the Tribal Law and Policy Institute in West Hollywood, California, the basic problem is that not only is prosecution of cases declined, no notification or reason is given for declining the case. The Institute works with the tribes for the development of justice programs. Mr. Gardner further added that the federal system takes a lot of time to arrive at a decision. When the case is as severe as sexual assault on a child, the message that comes across to the community is that no corrective action is being taken.

According to federal law, tribal courts possess the authority for prosecuting members of the tribe for committing crimes on reservations, but the maximum punishment that they can enforce is that of three years in jail. Therefore the tribes have no choice but to request federal prosecution when severe crimes are committed.

Dissatisfaction with the state of affairs has grown significantly to the extent that a number of tribal members have actually sued the government for refusing to prosecute cases and, according to them, incompetent police work.

In 2012, a federal court in the state of Montana gave permission to Steven Bearcrane's family to sue an FBI agent. According to the family, the agent conducted a homicide investigation into the death of their son, which was flawed. There was an additional accusation in the lawsuit that stated that it was commonplace for the office of the United States attorney to reject cases of crime in which Native Indians were the victims.

The Justice Department claims to have improved in its resolution of conflicts with the tribes. As evidence, the department pointed out the Tribal Law and Order Act, which had been agreed upon by Congress in 2010, for the strengthening of systems for tribal law enforcement, and the directive that had been issued to US attorneys for working more closely with the leaders of the tribes.

However, according to Tao Etpison, who was a former judge belonging to the Tonto Apaches in Arizona, the federal prosecutors usually work on the cases several hundred miles away from the relevant reservation. There have been several times when the justification of the decision of the Justice Department to decline the prosecution of a case was US attorneys suffering from lack of resources. According to Mr. Etpison, the crimes create grave implications for the reservation, which the federal prosecutors do not perceive from the perspective of the reservation.

In 2011, 52% of the cases which involved the most severe criminal offenses committed on

Native Indian reservations were not filed by federal prosecutors. These figures were acquired by the Transactional Records Access Clearinghouse at Syracuse University. The institution can recover federal data under the Freedom of Information Act.

65% of the rape charges that had arisen on reservations in 2011, were not pursued by the government. 61% of the cases that involved sexual abuse charges on children were rejected by the government. On the other hand, only 20% of the cases that involved drug trafficking on a nationwide basis were declined by the Justice Department. These are the figures according to federal data.

According to the Office of Government Accountability, once a case is declined by federal prosecutors, the evidence is seldom handed over to the tribal courts. According to another report, federal prosecutors do not even notify the relevant tribes once they have decided to decline cases until the statute of limitations for the tribe has finished.

As a response, federal prosecutors state that they make a full effort to provide as much information as they can to the tribes about declined cases. However, they are limited often because of the possibility of reopening the cases later on.

According to Kerry J. Jacobson who is an assistant US attorney in Wyoming, the undertaking of tribal prosecutions during the time the government is taking a decision on whether to file charges or not, would only result in further problems and complications.

She said that they wouldn't be in a position to provide their evidence while they were still conducting their investigation and that she would not want that a sexual assault be made to testify two times.

Unfortunately however, the victims do not provide testimony at all.

According to Mr. Etpison, federal prosecutors had declined the pursuit of around 40 cases of sexual assault in the recent years. Most of the cases had involved children.

According to Thomas W. Weissmuller, who has been a chief judge for many tribes, he had been the judge in case of a trial that took place on the Swinomish Reservation in the state of Washington. The case involved a man who was 31 years old and had mixed root beer schnapps in the root beer for a girl who was 13 years old. Unaware of the mix, the girl had consumed the soda and passed out. The man had covered her face with her own clothes and proceeded to rape her.

Mr. Weissmuller stated that despite a DNA match and the corroboration from two relatives who had interrupted the attack, federal prosecutors had declined to file charges.

Even though the tribal court had convicted the man of rape, he served only a year in prison, which was the maximum penalty allowed in the tribal system's law at that time. The Justice Department declined from discussing the case.

Mr. Weissmuller stated that he didn't understand why there wasn't a federal prosecution as he believed that the case was completely clear cut.

Substance abuse

American Indians (AIs) have endured poor health, high mortality rates and psychopathology due to their impoverished economic conditions. Substance abuse has been the chief causal factor in the poor health outcomes. Studies show higher statistics of substance abuse among American Indians than the American population as a whole.

Alcohol and tobacco abuse have increased infant mortality rates among American Indians. American Indian women consumed more tobacco and alcohol while expecting, at rates that were higher than the national rate. In fact, problems related to substance abuse, including cirrhosis and liver diseases, are among the top ten causes that account for a high number of deaths.

According to studies, alcoholism is a major issue among American Indians. In 1987, nearly 19% Indian death were because of alcohol, which stood greater than the US average of 4.7%. Alcoholism is divided into various behaviors, including: binge-drinking, alcohol abuse and alcohol dependency. Alcoholism has been the leading cause for health troubles and mortality rates. Literature suggests that more sicknesses and injuries result from alcohol than other behaviors.

There are several factors that explain high alcohol-related deaths among American-Indians. First, there are demographic factors that affect alcohol-related deaths. Data shows a high number of deaths from alcoholism among the young American Indian population. Second, geography has also affected alcohol-related deaths. Since a large number of Indians reside in suburban regions and reservations outside states, there are a high number of deaths due to lack of access to healthcare, poverty, environment and crime. Furthermore, legal, social, economic and political worsen alcohol problems. Majority of the Indians are poor;

therefore, lack of privileges and access to services affect their behavior. Even tribal customs have exacerbated alcohol abuse. Since education levels among American Indians are low, Indians are usually unaware of safety rules and regulations.

Since American-Indian communities live in reservations, each community has its own policies due to which alcohol-consumption patterns and characteristics vary. Alcohol consumption patterns also change due to education levels and social status. Drinking patterns vary across different tribal communities. The Navajo community has reported the highest rates of drinking patterns and alcohol consumption keeps rising. The trends also show differences in drinking patterns among Indian adults and young population.

Heavy drinkers consume more than five drinks in a given situation and experience blackouts. In severe cases, when they engage in illegal activities out of intoxication, they have to face imprisonment or wide-ranging issues, such as high mortality or morbidity. Males drink alcohol in a higher proportion compared to females.

Research discovered a high association between alcohol and drug abuse and health implications. Literature suggests that race, afro-centricity, parental attachment, stress, trauma and religion have been the determining causes of substance abuse. AIs have suffered from traumatic stress as a result of hostilities, discriminatory attitudes, resentment, everyday difficulties, crimes, child abuse, culture and past history.

Alcohol consumption among AIs varied over the years by region and tribes. Urban tribes reported higher rates of substance abuse than rural populations. Alcohol is the most widely abused substance by AIs. More than 95% boys and girls had begun alcohol consumption by 12th grade. AIs were prone to starting alcohol consumption earlier, in greater proportions and suffering from serious health risks. Studies found high rates of alcohol consumption among the AI youth. Alcohol abuse rates among eight graders were double than the rates of other ethnic and white populations.

The rates of drinking among AI youth were reportedly higher than whites, blacks, Hispanics and Asian Americans. AIs were more susceptible to perishing due to alcohol abuse than non-AIs. A study classified AI alcohol drinkers into recreational drinkers and anxiety drinkers. Recreational drinkers were those who drank at workplaces, night parties, away from home or during the weekends. Females engage in this type of drinking pattern but in lesser proportion than males. As for anxiety drinkers, they were mostly those who were marginalized and could not find employment; therefore, they were chronic drinkers. Mostly, the male population fit this drinking pattern and were excluded from both the Indian and non-Indian communities. They drink both while being in company and alone. They usually spend time in row areas or border towns of western states. Recreational and anxiety drinkers are characterized by alcohol-abusive and alcohol-specific problems. Anxiety drinkers usually die of liver cirrhosis, other alcohol-related health issues and vehicle accidents. Recreational drinkers are responsible for mostly accidental or suicide deaths.

More Indians die from alcohol-related deaths, for instance suicide, vehicle accidents and homicide. American-natives are known for their alcohol-abusive and alcohol-dependent attitudes. The youth is divided into peer cluster of heavy, recreational or anxiety drinkers. The tribal customs do not discourage them from drinking alcohol. They don't raise awareness about the risks and health complications related to alcohol consumption. They encourage mixing in risky environments, behavioral patterns, drunk driving and aggression.

A study showed that most of the child abuse cases in American native communities were related to alcohol abuse. In New Mexico, around 93% of child abuse and child neglect cases were due to alcohol consumption and the problem continued in many families, for several generations.

Drug abuse, particularly use of cocaine and marijuana was common among AI youth, with prevalence of lifetime abuse for smokeless tobacco and cigarettes. The rates of drug abuse keep increasing AI students. Adolescents between 13 and 17 years showed the highest rates for illicit drug use.

Furthermore, AIs have suffered from psychopathologies, such as depression, anxiety and post-traumatic stress disorder, resulting from substance abuse. Depression was widespread among urban AI communities, specifically those who lacked education. Women with histories of alcohol dependency reported greater rates of anxiety, phobia, depression, psychoses and obsessive compulsive behaviors.

Studies also show that AI substance abusers engaged in risky sexual behaviors that often led to HIV infection. They engaged in unsafe behaviors in exchange for money or drugs. AI drug users were found to drink to the point of intoxication and engage in risky behaviors during blackout.

Historical trauma among AIs usually resulted from past aggression towards AIs, colonial authority, forced relocation from homeland and placing AI children into custodial care. AIs had been oppressed and disempowered at the hands of colonial leaders. This trauma has become embedded in the collective consciousness of AI community and has also had negative health, social and psychological implications, for instance, depression, mortality rates, grief, alienation cardiovascular diseases and survivor's guilt.

When it comes to violence, AIs have been at the receiving end since they have been treated with repulsion and aggression. A study showed that AIs were more vulnerable to violent crimes than the national average rates reported. They were more prone than other ethnic groups to experience sexual assaults and interracial violence, by both whites and blacks.

AIs have also testified to traumatic life incidents due to accidents, overdose, rape and gun violence. The victims reported higher rates of PTSD and other mental illnesses. Those AIs who had experienced a higher number of traumatic life events were more susceptible to substance abuse. A positive association was found between trauma and substance abuse, indicating the greater the trauma, the greater the likelihood of substance abuse.

Moreover, those AI children who had been maltreated or sexually abused were likely to begin substance abuse as they grew up. Mostly, AI children were removed from their homes and placed in blind adoption homes. The number of out-of-home AI children continues to rise. There was a significant association between child abuse and alcohol consumption – the greater the abuse, the higher the consumption (Walters, Simoni, & Evans-Campbell, 2002).

Sexual abuse and violence

Imperial governments of Europe and America have been oppressing American Indians for many years in domains including: economic privileges, religion and education. American-Indian (AI) youth are prone to engaging in risky sexual behaviors due to historical trauma, grief, childhood abuse, antagonism and substance abuse. AI drug users tend to engage in a higher number of risky behaviors in exchange for drugs or money. Users drank alcohol or abused drugs until intoxicated and engaged in unprotected sexual behaviors. There has been an increase HIV and other health behaviors that result from unsafe sexual behaviors.

Sexual violence against women and children is common within AI communities. This is mostly used as a method for domination and control and by treating the victims as objects or inferiors. Those groups who were marginalized on the basis of their race, gender and class also experience violence due to male chauvinism. Women and children of color are more vulnerable to violence and are devalued within the society.

Moreover, an increase in risky sexual behaviors has led to a rise in teenage pregnancies. In 2007, pregnancies among native Indians had increased by 12%, which was higher than the national rates. Teenage girls of Novajo tribe reported the highest pregnancy rates.

A study showed that teenagers had begun having intercourse by 12th grade. Adolescents in middle and high school reported that they did not use protection. Other reports indicated variances in teenage pregnancy. Therefore, AIs are more likely to engage in unprotected intercourse at younger age and in greater proportion than other ethnicities.

Sexual abuse is an outcome of wide-ranging factors among AIs. They are among the most socially, economically and culturally disempowered communities in USA. Due to poverty, lack of privileges in jobs and education and broken marriages, children exhibit retarded physical and mental development.

A survey showed that 34% American Indian had been raped or experienced attempted rape, which was greater than white, African-American and Asian-American women. Nonetheless, the justice system prosecutes few sex offenders. Not all of the offenders are arrested. This is because mostly, AI women are afraid of reporting the act because that would bring shame to their tribes, particularly if non-natives are involved. Native also report distrust in the courts to prosecute offenders. If assaults are reported to the courts, there is no guarantee that justice would be carried out.

The authorities either ignore the offence or take hours or day to file a report and prosecute the perpetrator. AI women cannot rely on state protection. Even tribal governments do not have jurisdiction to take action against non-natives. Therefore, most of the offenders go unpunished.

The forms of violence that are usually carried out against AI women include: beating, rape, assault and coercion. Most of these offences are carried out by non-Native men; thus, leaving women more vulnerable to attacks. The tribal justice systems do not receive funding from the state. A combination of these factors aggravates incidents of sexual abuse and violence.

Even though the Violence Against Women Act was enacted in 2013 and gave authority to tribal governments to prosecute non-natives, it did not cover crimes of rape, child sexual abuse and assaults. Once the law was implemented in 2015, a few tribal governments still lacked the resources and jurisdiction to prosecute offenders.

A recent report showed that most of the offenders against tribal communities were white. Furthermore, each person had experienced some form of interracial violence. The tribal governments may prosecute the offenders but they still cannot provide adequate protection to the victims. Restraining orders are not always implemented because of lack of willingness of tribal governments to work with the state.

Child sexual abuse is also common among American Indian tribes. Children, especially from dysfunctional households and socially disorganized groups are victimized to a great extent. The traumatic experiences are known to lead to substance abuse and psychopathologies in adolescence and adulthood (Robin, Chester, Rasmussen, Jaranson, & Goldman, 1997).

The effects of childhood abuse continue into adulthood and increase risks of sexual abuse, substance abuse or mental disorders. This leaves adolescents vulnerable to teenage pregnancies and life-threatening illnesses. Childhood abuse among AIs increased due to high alcohol consumption, poverty and economic deprivation. It also contributes to powerlessness, stigma and disorders (Hobfoll, Anita Bansal, & Pierce, 2002).

Poverty

American Indians are among the smallest minorities and also the poorest groups in America. One in four families earn below the poverty line. The burden of poverty is felt by better-off Indians as well. American Indians mostly reside in rural areas, on reservation lands outside metropolitan areas. Since Indians were forcibly removed from their homelands, they scattered throughout the continent. When the US population increased, AIs were seen with repugnance and considered as impediments to economic development.

The white people tried removing Indians from white lands and this led to disputes that often ended in bloodshed. Indians were forced to give up their traditions and relocate. Therefore, AIs have been among the most disenfranchised groups in America.

AIs have been deprived of opportunities in job, education and socio-cultural sectors. There are discrepancies in incomes, education and employment among AI tribes. AI children usually lag behind at school and have high dropout rates. A large majority is unemployed and unable to support families.

The issue is that poverty has led to widespread crime among Indian reservations. There is an association between poverty and crime, indicating that the higher the poverty rate, the greater the crime rate. A report showed that poverty rates among Indians are higher than the national average and lesser than urban poverty rate.

Tribal AI communities are trapped in a vicious cycle of poverty: they are born into poor households and are unable to get access to quality healthcare and education services. Thus, they are deprived of market opportunities and cannot sustain themselves. Therefore, they remain poor, semi- or unskilled and in poor health. The cycle continues for generations.

Since they lack privileges to live a good-quality life, they seek employment in black markets or turn to substance abuse, violence and criminal activities. The worst crimes are reported in Detroit, Flint and Michigan. Even though US has a robust police force and judicial system, the state has been unable to provided resources to prosecute the offenders or address the underlying causes of crime.

Studies show high rates of crime and violence among AI tribes but the statistics are not representative of all tribal communities. The results usually depict crime rates outside tribes and reservation lands. The sample used in the report is not representative of all households.

According to a census conducted in 2012, Indian Reservations were among the top five poorest counties. Some tribes even reported unemployment rates soaring as high as 85%. Tribal governments only offer jobs in social services, health services and schools. They have limited resources to provide economics opportunities. The government also isolated the people from fertile lands and water sources.

Native Americans have the lowest employment rate compared to other ethnic groups. Only one-third of the men were employed in full – time jobs. The students from these communities record lower scores on arithmetic. The tribes have the lowest graduation rates since students drop out due to lack of finances. The reservations have a greater percentage of houses than the entire US. The houses are deprived of clean water and sanitation. The reservations do not have well-developed infrastructure, roads and bridges, which are mostly useless.

Policy-makers are working to provide educational services and business prospects. Some American Indians have also established their own charity organizations to improve basic infrastructure, social, health and educational services.

Conclusion

Studies show that culture, social mobility and economic status play a role in influencing drinking behavior or abuse among the American-Indian population. Bicultural individuals were found to be heavier drinkers than other American-Indian communities. Alcohol has been the leading cause of health complications and mental disorders.

Even though there are wide-ranging problems in Indian reservations, Indian communities have undertaken efforts to regulate vices, improve infrastructure and provide access to education and healthcare. The tribal governments have arrested perpetrators and prohibited sale of liquor in some areas.

Some American-Indians have participated in initiatives to raise their voice through writing and art. The Four World's initiative was taken to involve tribal leaders in the decision-making process, encourage individual participation, establish community organizations and take action. Similarly, the Community Partnership Program was facilitated to raise awareness about substance abuse and develop preventative strategies to counteract alcohol or drug abuse.

Health personnel have undertaken efforts at primary, secondary and tertiary levels to combat substance abuse. In primary prevention, measures are taken to prevent onset of substance abuse, starting at preschools and elementary schools. To accomplish this, tribal leaders have initiated reservation treatment and anger management programs. The target for primary prevention includes school-going youth. In secondary prevention, measures are undertaken to prevent the problems from getting worse. Intervention programs are directed at youth who have begun consuming alcohol and to prevent them from engaging in further self-destructive behaviors. Tertiary prevention is directed to cure deviant behavior. Recovery programs and holistically-designed to help individuals get rid of substance abuse.   The abuses the Native American Indians have throughout the forming of this Country has been close to an almost genocide approach to the indigenous people. The Draconian approach to Law Enforcement of Federal Law has had a very heavy detrimental effect on what is fair and appropriate in executing punishment for violations of law that if were govern by state law, would be nowhere near the level of severity. Crimes committed by none natives on native lands are not taken or looked upon as that serious.

The torment of time and lack of decency shown to the AI is beyond reproach.

The AI voice seems to never be heard. History had depicted the AI as wild and for them to be treated like cattle being forced to move to Reservations like animals on the plains. The lack of support to the AI reservations is well beyond what third world countries get. I could also go as far as the US Government takes better care of people from other countries then they do here. It is unknown what the future holds, but one thing is for sure, is that the Native Americans will be there.

www.ingramcontent.com/pod-product-compliance
Lightning Source LLC
Chambersburg PA
CBHW071124030426
42336CB00013BA/2201